How to Meditate:

Diverse Mindfulness Techniques and Concentration Practices

NICOL MORALES

Contents

Introduction: Why Do We Live? 1

    The Enemy Within and the Path to Purification 1

    The Parable of the Mirror 3

    What is Meditation? 3

    Meditation as a Path to Clarity 4

    Meditation as a Path to Understanding the Meaning of Life 5

Chapter 01: The History of Meditation 8

    Meditation in Ancient Times 8

    Medieval Traditions and Philosophical Reflections 11

    The Revival of Meditation in Western Culture 12

    Meditation in Our Time: Salvation in an Age of Overload 13

Chapter 02: Meditation in the Digital Age 15

    A Story of the Master and His Disciples 16

    Meditation and Digital Detox 17

    Morning: Create Space for Yourself 19

    Mindful Breaks throughout the Day 20

    Evening: A Time for Gratitude 21

    Small Steps Toward Big Change 22

Chapter 03: Scientific Research on Meditation 23

Chapter 04: Energy, Chakras, and Connection with the Universe 26

    Humans as Energy Systems 26

    Chakras: Centers of Energy and Their Roles 26

    Meditation on Chakras: The Key to Harmony 29

Chapter 0531Main Types of Meditation **31**

    Breath Meditation (Anapana, Pranayama) 31

    Nadi Shodhana (Alternate Nostril Breathing) 32

    Sound Meditation (Nada Yoga) 35

    Meditation on Visualization (Trataka, Visualization) 38

    Advanced Visualization Meditations 41

Chapter 06:Meditation in Daily Life and Relationships ....
48

    Meditation in Everyday Activities 48

    Meditation for Inner Harmony 53

    Meditations for Relationships 58

Chapter 07:Transcendental Meditation: The Path to the Divine ..
67

    Immersion into the Transcendental State 67

    Mantras: The Key to Deep Awareness 67

    __Examples of Transcendental Mantras 69

Chapter 08:The Power of Sacred Names ....
72

    The Bhagavad Gita on Meditation 72

    A Journey Through Ages 74

    Satya Yuga 75

    Treta Yuga 77

    Dvapara Yuga 78

    Kali Yuga 80

    The Power of Sound 83

Lord Chaitanya 84

The Impact of Mantra Meditation on Modern Culture and Society . 86

The Holy Name: A Guide to Spiritual Transformation 89

The Uniqueness of the "Hare Krishna" Mantra 90

Types and Techniques of Mantra Meditation 91

Japa (Personal Meditation with the Mantra) 91

Kirtan (Collective Chanting) 92

Harinama: 94

Chapter 09: Practical Tips for Building a Sustainable Daily Practice 96

Tips for Building a Sustainable Daily Practice 96

Conclusion 98

Introduction: Why Do We Live?

The Enemy Within and the Path to Purification

If you ask people the question, "Why do we live?", the answers will be as diverse as the people themselves. Some will say they live for love, others for happiness, family, or self-realization. But what if our path to these goals is blocked? What if there is an enemy that prevents us from moving forward?

And this enemy is not outside; it is deep within us. It is our inner "dirt": fears, worries, anger, greed, and envy. These are precisely the things that keep us from finding peace and understanding ourselves.

These states capture our consciousness and lead us astray. We mistakenly believe that happiness will come from money or success, that defeating external enemies will bring us peace. But chasing these illusions takes us further and further away from the truth.

Every day, we face countless sources of stress: the endless stream of tasks, external circumstances, and our own inner worries. Stress permeates our consciousness, creating constant state of tension that is difficult to escape. In such conditions, meditation becomes a lifeline. It allows us to slow down, disconnect from the chaos of the outer world, and restore our connection with ourselves. Meditation not only helps to release accumulated stress but also teaches us to avoid accumulating it, helping us to perceive life with greater ease and clarity.

Imagine a dark room in which you find yourself. You've stood there for a long time, very long. Over time, your imagination begins to draw monsters and creatures hiding in the corners. It seems that danger lurks at every step.

But then you find a small candle. Its light fills the room, dispelling the darkness. And what do you see? There are no monsters, no creatures—just you, standing in an empty space.

And so it is in life. The darkness represents our fears and anxieties. They are but illusions created by our mind. And only awareness, this inner light, allows us to see the truth.

Every person encounters such enemies. For some, it is the fear of failure; for others, it's worries about the future; for still others, it is anger filling the heart to the brim. All these states act like dirt, covering our true "self", like a foggy glass through which it's impossible to see the beauty of the world.

But can we cleanse ourselves of this? Of course, yes. And the journey begins with realizing that our enemy is not the external world but our own thoughts.

The Parable of the Mirror

A man once came to a wise sage and said: "Teacher, I cannot find peace. My mind is full of fears, anxieties, and anger."

The sage rose, took out an old mirror covered with a thick layer of dust, and handed it to the man. "Look—what do you see?"

The man frowned. "Nothing. This mirror is too dirty."

The sage smiled. "Your mind is just like this mirror. It is covered in layers of dirt — fears, envy, anger. But if you start cleaning it, layer by layer, you will eventually see your true reflection. It is pure, clear, and peaceful."

The man reflected on the sage's words and realized that his peace depended solely on how diligently he worked to clean his inner mirror.

The sage may not have spoken the word "meditation," but his lesson was entirely about it.

What is Meditation?

The term "meditation" comes from the Latin word *meditation*, meaning "reflection" or "contemplation." However, its significance goes far beyond simple reflection. In spiritual practice, meditation is conscious contemplation aimed at achieving inner peace and harmony. It is a path to connection with the higher "self" or with the Divine.

From a philosophical perspective, meditation is deep reflection, a search for truth, an attempt to understand the nature of things and find answers to the most important questions.

In the modern world, meditation is increasingly perceived as a tool for relaxation and stress relief. It is a way to restore inner balance amidst the rapid pace of life.

But regardless of the meaning you assign to meditation, its goal remains unchanged: purification.

Meditation as a Path to Clarity

Meditation is the process that helps us remove the layers of "dirt" that prevent us from seeing clearly. What holds us back are the habitual beliefs rooted in our consciousness: "You can't," "You're not good enough," "You don't deserve happiness…"

These thoughts are invisible barriers that bind us hand and foot. We live according to false ideals, trying to meet others' expectations, or get stuck in the race for perfection, which always remains elusive.

Meditation allows us to see these barriers, to expose their illusory nature, and to free ourselves from their power. It is like the light of a lantern or candle, illuminating the dark corners of our consciousness and helping us realize that all these limitations are merely creations of our own minds.

Life gains clarity, like a reflection on the calm surface of a lake. When consciousness is purified, it becomes easier to understand why we live.

Not to fight external enemies, not to accumulate possessions. But to be in harmony with ourselves and the world.

Meditation helps us remember that our true reflection has always been pure and clear. We just need to have the courage to wipe away the dust, layer by layer, and allow ourselves to see the light.

Meditation as a Path to Understanding the Meaning of Life

Meditation is not just a relaxation technique. It is a meeting with yourself, deep and honest. In a state of relaxation, we begin to understand that the fears that grip us are merely shadows of our thoughts. We see that anger, envy, and greed are not who we are but temporary emotions that come and go.

Each time we sit in silence, it's as if we rise above the noise of our lives. At first, it's not easy: thoughts shout, demand attention. But if we continue, we will feel the noise subside. One by one, worries fade away, and clarity and peace open before us.

Just as a lotus grows in muddy water, remaining pure, so too does our soul, surrounded by fears and doubts, retain its purity. The lotus reaches for the light, overcoming the dirt around it, and unfolds, symbolizing purity and harmony.

Life gains meaning when we realize that its essence lies in the process of growth itself, in being true to our nature despite external circumstances. We begin to understand that everything we need is already within us: strength, peace, love, and harmony.

When we cleanse our minds through meditation, the meaning of life becomes simple and clear: to live in harmony with ourselves, to follow our path, and to allow our soul to unfold like a lotus towards the light of truth and awareness. The goal of meditation is to calm the mind because when the noise of thoughts subsides, a person gains the ability to see the world as it truly is, not distorted by prejudices and worries. In this state of clarity and peace, we learn not just to be here and now—we discover our inner nature.

Meditation develops concentration—the ability to direct attention to a single point, to be fully immersed in the present. This practice allows us to see the subtlest, hidden aspects of reality. Like a beam of light penetrating the darkness, meditation awakens intuition, opening doors to knowledge beyond ordinary senses.

When the mind attains peace and focus, the opportunity arises to go beyond the limitations of the material world. Suffering no longer holds a person captive. The inner world becomes boundless, and you realize that everything happening in the outer world merely reflects your consciousness. Meditation brings freedom from fears, attachments, and limitations, opening the path to the infinite, to your true nature.

In this book, we will embark on an exciting journey to ourselves. Step by step, we will learn simple but profound practices that help us cleanse our consciousness.

Through meditation, we will learn not only to calm the mind and relieve stress but also to hear our true desires and find answers to the most important questions. Why do we live? What is our purpose? How can we experience true happiness?

This book will guide you on the path to a conscious, harmonious, and fulfilling life.

Chapter 01 The History of Meditation

Meditation in Ancient Times

Meditation is an ancient practice that has existed in various cultures and among many peoples. Its origins are lost in the depths of time when humanity lived in close connection with nature and sought to understand its role in the universe. Even then, meditation served as a means for people to find answers to profound questions about life and death, the meaning of existence, and their interaction with higher powers.

One of the oldest traditions of meditation comes from India. The Vedic texts describe meditation practices as a way to connect with the Divine. Yogis and sages used meditation to achieve *Samadhi*—a state of unity with the Absolute.

Sitting by the banks of sacred rivers or in the shadows of mountain peaks, they practiced breathing techniques and contemplation, observing their thoughts and emotions until their minds became completely still. Their bodies remained motionless, as if they had become part of the surrounding nature. In the silence of the jungles, only the rustle of leaves and the sound of sacred waters accompanied their practices. They sought answers within themselves, delving deeper into the mysteries of existence. In this state, they found true freedom— freedom from suffering and the illusions of the material world.

Shamans of northern tribes, dressed in animal skins, sat by fires on cold nights, entering a trance to connect with the spirits of nature and ancestors. To the sounds of drums and whispers of the wind, they ventured into the invisible realm where the boundaries between the physical and spiritual worlds dissolved. In such moments, they saw the world as it truly was, realizing that all living beings were interconnected.

In the arid deserts of the Middle East, Sufi mystics practiced their forms of meditation, known as *dhikr*. Spinning in rhythmic dances and repeating the sacred names of God, they sought to dissolve themselves in divine love.

In Ancient Egypt, beneath the grandeur of the pyramids, priests and mystics delved into deep meditative states. They believed that meditation opened the gates to the afterlife and helped them understand the nature of the soul. In the dimly lit temple halls, illuminated only by flickering torches, they sat in silence, contemplating the symbolism of their gods and gaining higher wisdom and harmony.

In Tibet, among snow-covered mountains, Buddhist monks sought enlightenment through meditation. In secluded monasteries, accompanied by the sounds of mantras and prayer bells, they practiced *Vipassana* and *Dzogchen*. These practices helped them achieve the state of *shunyata*— emptiness, liberation from attachments, and suffering.

Indigenous peoples of North and South America—Incas, Mayans, and shamans—used meditation in rituals related to natural cycles and cosmic phenomena. Through deep concentration and immersion, they communicated with the spirits of the earth and sky.

At the dawn of Western civilization, meditative practices found their reflection in the philosophy of Ancient Greece. Although the Greeks did not use the term "meditation" as we know it today, their approaches to reflection and contemplation laid the foundation for similar practices. Pythagoras, the renowned philosopher and mathematician, taught his students the art of contemplative living, which included periodic retreats, silence, and inner self-discovery. The Pythagoreans believed that deep immersion in thought could bring harmony with the cosmos.

Plato and Socrates also promoted the ideas of inner contemplation as a way to understand truth. For them, true knowledge was linked not only to the external world but also to the internal world, accessible through immersion in thought. Plato argued that through internal dialogue, one could reach the world of ideas—a spiritual reality beyond the material world.

In Ancient Rome, meditation was reflected in philosophical schools like Stoicism. Marcus Aurelius, a Roman emperor and philosopher, used meditative techniques of self-analysis to understand his mind and grasp moral principles. In his work *Meditations*, one can find examples of contemplative practices aimed at developing self-control, calmness, and detachment from material concerns. The Stoics taught mental discipline and inner focus, striving to control emotions and live in harmony with nature.

The primary goal of Christian meditation was and remains to connect with God through prayerful reflection, dialogue with the Divine, and understanding biblical truths.

Medieval Traditions and Philosophical Reflections

With the onset of the Enlightenment and the growing influence of science and reason on Western society, interest in meditation as a spiritual practice temporarily waned. However, philosophers continued to ponder the nature of consciousness and the inner world of humans. René Descartes, for instance, in his famous work *Meditations on First Philosophy*, used methodical doubt as a form of mental meditation to understand the foundations of existence and truth.

During this period, meditation took a backseat as philosophers and scientists focused on rational inquiry and explaining the laws of the surrounding world through logic.

The Revival of Meditation in Western Culture

From the late 19th to early 20th century, meditation returned to the West with renewed vigor, thanks to the growing interest in Eastern spiritual traditions. Western thinkers and scholars began actively studying Indian philosophy, Buddhism, and Taoism. During this period, the Theosophical Society, founded by Helena Blavatsky, popularized the ideas of Eastern mysticism and meditation among Western audiences.

In the mid-20th century, meditation gained widespread popularity, thanks to spiritual leaders like Swami Vivekananda and Paramahansa Yogananda, who traveled to the West, bringing the traditions of Indian yoga and meditation. Yogananda, in particular, authored the famous book *Autobiography of a Yogi*, which inspired millions of Western readers to explore meditation.

In the 1960s, meditation experienced a true boom in the West, thanks to Maharishi Mahesh Yogi and Srila Prabhupada. Each of them was deeply inspired by ancient Indian spiritual traditions.

Meditation in Our Time: Salvation in an Age of Overload

Our era is one of endless haste and informational noise, where each day brings new challenges and stresses. We are surrounded by streams of data, demands, and expectations, and this pressure is sometimes so overwhelming that even a brief moment of peace feels like a luxury. In this chaos, it is easy to lose oneself, to lose touch with who we truly are, and to forget that true happiness and peace come not from external sources but from within. In such conditions, spiritual purification becomes the only salvation.

Each of us has experienced the feeling of exhaustion when stress tightens its grip, and the mind becomes flooded with a whirlwind of thoughts and worries. These invisible chains gradually drain our life force, turning each day into a struggle for survival. But meditation is not resistance—it is liberation. It's like taking a deep breath of fresh air after being in a stuffy room for too long. Through this practice, we find purification from accumulated tension and from everything that depletes our energy and destroys our inner harmony.

Now more than ever, we need to pause and look inward. For it is only through inner transformation that we can confront the challenges of the modern world. Meditation is the bridge to this state. It helps a person break free from illusions and return to their true nature.

Chapter 02 Meditation in the Digital Age

We live in a world where time fades under the glow of screens. From morning to late evening, notifications, social media feeds, messages, work tasks, and emails flood our minds, leaving no room for silence and peace. Like an endless river of information, the digital flow sweeps us into its depths, and often don't even realize how exhausting it is to fight against its current. The digital age has become a new challenge for the human mind, robbing us not only of tranquility but also of the ability to focus on a single task.

In such a world, meditation is like an island amid the stormy waves of the information ocean. It offers not just rest but a profound awareness of how we've become entangled in the chaos of thoughts and actions. Through meditation, we learn to slow down, become present in the moment, break free from the endless cycle of notifications, and reconnect with ourselves.

A Story of the Master and His Disciples

In a distant monastery, there lived an old master renowned for his wisdom and deep tranquility. One day, his disciples came to him and asked,

"Teacher, how can we find peace in this restless world? We cannot avoid work, interactions, and all these tasks, but we want to learn how to maintain inner balance."

The master led them to a river. The water rushed and roared, breaking against the rocks. The disciples expected the master to say something profound, but he simply sat on the riverbank and began observing the water. In silence, they sat for a long time until one disciple dared to ask,

"Teacher, what should we do? How can we stop the flow of this river?"

The master looked at him and replied, "You cannot stop the river. You cannot control its current. But you can learn to observe it while remaining at peace. It is the same with life: you cannot stop the flow of tasks and messages, but you can find silence within yourself."

This story reminds us that while digital overload is an external reality, our inner silence can remain constant. Meditation helps us stop fighting the current and instead become observers, maintaining peace even amidst the chaos of the digital world.

Meditation and Digital Detox

When our body is overloaded with toxins, exhausted and weakened, we turn to detox—a cleansing process. We give up unhealthy food and reconsider our habits to allow the body to recover, free itself from excess, and regain health.

But in today's world, it's not just our body that needs cleansing—our mind does too. The constant strain on our minds caused by the endless race for news and tasks makes disconnecting from technology just as crucial.

A Digital detox is a process that helps our mind free itself from the noise and tension we often fail to notice. It's not just about temporarily giving up phones and computers—it's a conscious decision to pause, slow down, and allow ourselves to recover. This detox is a way to cleanse the mind, reclaim focus, and rediscover joy in simple things.

Setting aside your laptop or phone for a while and starting your day with a moment of peace instead of checking notifications, news, and messages is an act of digital detox.
This step helps you regain control over your attention.

This simple act transforms the morning. Instead of being overwhelmed by notifications, you experience silence. Instead of rushing, you take a deep breath. Instead of engaging in a senseless race for information, you gain clarity about what truly matters to you.

Every time we grab our phone, we give our attention to something that often doesn't value it. But what if we dedicated that time to ourselves? Let the present moment become your priority. Feel the noise fade away and peace take its place.

Let's begin now, with just one minute of silence. Soon, we'll notice how this habit transforms our lives. This isn't about rejecting technology forever—it's about reclaiming control over our attention and ceasing to be prisoners of screens.

Living more mindfully and incorporating breaks from gadgets into daily life is simpler than it seems. All it takes is a bit of patience, a few small steps, and the desire to make life calmer and brighter.

Morning: Create Space for Yourself

Try starting your day with a pause. Resist the urge to grab your phone immediately upon waking. Instead, take a few moments to sit quietly. Make yourself a cup of tea or coffee, feel the warmth of the mug in your hands, inhale the aroma of the drink, and listen to the world waking up around you.

If time allows, dedicate a few minutes to meditation. This could be as simple as observing your breath. Close your eyes and focus on the air entering and leaving your lungs. Let thoughts come and go without clinging to them. Gradually, your mind will calm, and you'll feel clarity and lightness.

Mindful Breaks throughout the Day

The hustle and rhythm of the day often carry us away, leaving little time for rest. But even amid tasks, you can find moments to reset. For instance, during a lunch break or between tasks, pause for a minute. Instead of reaching for your phone, close your eyes and take a deep breath.

Notice your body—where do you feel tension? Is your mind at rest?

These small anchors help you return to the present moment. You stop operating on autopilot and begin noticing what's happening here and now.

Evening: A Time for Gratitude

   The evening is a time to let go of everything that has accumulated throughout the day. Try turning off gadgets an hour before bedtime. Leave your phone in another room and turn off the TV. Instead, light a candle, dim the lights, and immerse yourself in silence.

Spend a few minutes reflecting on gratitude. Recall something you can say "thank you" for from the day that has passed. Perhaps it was a stranger's smile, a sunny day, or a cup of your favorite tea. These simple moments help you end the day with lightness and peace.

Small Steps Toward Big Change

Start small: one morning without a phone, one mindful pause during the day, a few minutes of silence before bed.

That's enough to notice the first changes.

Even a temporary disconnection from modern technology restores balance, helps you regain control over thoughts, and makes moments without gadgets truly precious.

This is a path toward living here and now—fully, vividly, and mindfully.

Chapter 03 Scientific Research on Meditation

Meditation, long regarded as a practice for achieving inner peace, now has scientific validation of its effectiveness. Modern research has proven that meditation not only helps

manage stress but also causes tangible changes in the brain and body. Using technologies such as functional magnetic resonance imaging (fMRI) and electroencephalography (EEG), scientists have been able to study its effects on the human brain. The findings are remarkable. Research at Harvard University has shown that regular meditation practice increases gray matter density in the hippocampus, the brain region responsible for memory and learning. Additionally, meditation strengthen neural connections in the prefrontal cortex, enhancing focus, self-control, and decision-making skills.

Meditation also has a significant impact on emotional wellbeing. Studies at Oxford University confirmed that mindfulness practice helps individuals manage depression by reducing the likelihood of relapses. It decreases activity in brain regions associated with reactive emotions, such as anxiety and anger. This makes practitioners more emotionally resilient and helps them recover from stress more quickly.

Physical health benefits from meditation as well. Lowering cortisol levels—the stress hormone—helps normalize blood pressure and strengthen the immune system. Researchers at the University of Wisconsin-Madison have demonstrated that meditation enhances resistance to infections and accelerates recovery from stressful situations.

These findings confirm that meditation is a powerful tool for cultivating mindfulness, maintaining inner calm, and improving overall health. This ancient practice has now become an integral part of modern life, bridging spiritual tradition with scientific achievement.

Chapter 04 Energy, Chakras, and Connection with the Universe

Humans as Energy Systems

It has long been established that humans are composed of both a physical body and an energetic one. The subtle body is a complex system that connects us to the universe. Let's explore how meditation influences this invisible energy structure, linking one's inner world with the surrounding cosmos. This system consists of energy channels through which prana flows, and chakras—centers where this energy concentrates. When energy flows freely, we experience harmony, balance, and a connection with the universe. However, blockages in these channels can cause tension and feelings of disconnection.

Chakras: Centers of Energy and Their Roles

Meditation helps restore the flow of energy, activating the chakras, which act as gateways to a deeper connection with the world. Energy flows through these centers both into and out of us, linking our being with the universal energy stream.

This harmony on a subtle level allows us to feel unity with ourselves and everything around us.

Meditation is the key to a deep understanding of the energetic body, which consists of channels and chakras— energy centers that regulate our physical, emotional, and spiritual state. These flows of vital energy connect us to the surrounding world. When they are open, we feel harmony and unity. However, stress, worries, and the hustle of modern life often block these channels, depriving us of a sense of wholeness.

Through meditation, we can open these blocked flows. Chakras begin to function as portals through which the energy of the universe enters our body. Each chakra serves a unique purpose, maintaining balance between our inner and outer worlds:

- **Muladhara (Root Chakra):** Grounds us, creating a sense of stability and connection to the Earth.
- **Svadhisthana (Sacral Chakra):** Governs emotions, creativity, and the joy of life.
- **Manipura (Solar Plexus Chakra):** Strengthens personal power and confidence.
- **Anahata (Heart Chakra):** Connects us with love and compassion.
- **Vishuddha (Throat Chakra):** Enables the expression of thoughts and feelings, creating harmony with the world.
- **Ajna (Third Eye Chakra):** Enhances intuition and allows us to perceive beyond physical reality.
- **Sahasrara (Crown Chakra):** Connects us to higher consciousness, opening the path to unity with the universe.

Meditation on Chakras: The Key to Harmony

Chakra meditation begins by focusing on each energy center, visualizing its color, and sensing how its energy awakens. Start with Muladhara, the root chakra, imagining a bright red light connecting you to the Earth and providing stability. Then move to Svadhisthana, the sacral chakra, filling yourself with the orange energy of creativity and joy.

Continue to visualize the yellow light of Manipura, the solar plexus chakra, which fills you with confidence and strength. Then immerse yourself in the green light of Anahata, the heart chakra, opening you to love and compassion. The blue energy of Vishuddha, the throat chakra, activates self-expression and harmony. The indigo light of Ajna, the third eye chakra, unveils intuition and inner wisdom. Finally, the violet glow of Sahasrara connects you to higher consciousness and the infinite flow of the universe.

For this meditation, you can choose silence, soothing music, or the repetition of mantras. Silence helps you focus on sensations, music provides a gentle background for relaxation, and mantras activate energy in the chakras. For example:

- Muladhara: Chant "Lam"
- Svadhisthana: Chant "Vam"
- Manipura: Chant "Ram"
- Anahata: Chant "Yam"
- Vishuddha: Chant "Ham"
- Ajna: Chant "Sham"
- Sahasrara: Chant "Om"

It is essential to understand that when energy channels are open, we feel a deep unity with the universe and harmony within ourselves. Aligning with these energy flows restores balance, harmony, and a sense of connection to the vast, infinite creation.

Chapter 05 Main Types of Meditation

When you begin meditating, it's as if you're diving into the ocean of your inner world, and each time, a new depth unfolds. There are many meditative techniques, each revealing different aspects of your personality and consciousness. Let's explore them in detail to understand how and when they work.

Breath Meditation (Anapana, Pranayama)

Breath meditation is one of the simplest and most accessible ways to begin your meditative journey. This technique focuses on your breathing—a simple, natural process that is always with us. Breathing is the most natural thing we have. We don't think about it; it happens on its own, yet this is where its power lies. When you consciously focus on your breath, the mind slows down, like a rushing river that suddenly becomes calm, reflecting a clear sky without a single cloud.

Imagine yourself in a quiet place. It might be your room, a park, or even a balcony overlooking trees. You sit down, straighten your back, relax your shoulders, close your eyes, and start observing your breath. At first, it seems like nothing is happening—just inhale, exhale, inhale, exhale. But the longer you observe, the deeper you dive into the process. The breath becomes an anchor, grounding you in the present moment. All thoughts, worries, and concerns begin to fade into the background.

Each inhale feels like a sip of fresh air, filling your body with energy. Each exhale becomes an opportunity to let go of tension and relax. Your attention is completely absorbed in the sensation of air entering your nose, filling your lungs, and moving through your body. This creates a deep silence within. Continue for 5–10 minutes, letting your breath be the center of your attention.

Here are some examples of breath meditation techniques, along with their descriptions:

Nadi Shodhana (Alternate Nostril Breathing) This breathing technique focuses on cleansing energy channels and balancing the right and left sides of the body and brain.

How to practice:

- Sit in a comfortable position with a straight back.
- Use the thumb of your right hand to close your right nostril. Inhale through your left nostril.
- Close your left nostril with your ring finger and exhale through your right nostril.
- Now inhale through your right nostril, close it, and exhale through your left nostril.
- Repeat this alternating breathing technique for 5–10 minutes.

Uddiyana Bandha (Abdominal Lift)

This breathing technique activates internal organs and awakens energy. It also helps improve digestion and relieve abdominal tension.

How to practice:

- Stand upright with feet shoulder-width apart and knees slightly bent.
- Take a deep breath in, and as you exhale, pull your abdomen inward and upward toward your spine, creating a vacuum in your abdomen.
- Hold your breath for a few seconds, then relax and inhale.
- Repeat several times, focusing on sensations in the abdomen and spine.

Sama Vritti (Equal Breathing)

This breathing meditation focuses on balancing inhales and exhales, helping to stabilize the mind and calm the nervous system.

How to practice:

- Sit in a comfortable position with a straight back.
  Close your eyes and begin breathing deeply.
- Gradually equalize the duration of your inhales and exhales. For example, inhale for a count of four and exhale for a count of four.

- If comfortable, increase the count to six or eight, maintaining even breathing.
- Continue the practice for 5–10 minutes, focusing on the equality of your breaths.

Kapalabhati (Shining Skull)

This more active breathing technique focuses on quick exhalations through the nose. It energizes and clears the mind, helping to quickly restore concentration. It's an excellent technique for morning awakening and activating vitality.

How to practice:

- Sit with a straight back. Take a deep breath through your nose.
- Exhale quickly and sharply through your nose, pulling your abdomen inward. Inhalation happens passively, without effort.
- Continue quick exhalations rhythmically—about 20–30 exhalations in a row.
- Do several cycles and finish the meditation with a deep, relaxing inhale and exhale.

4-7-8 Breathing (Calming Breath)

This simple but effective breathing technique helps you quickly calm down, relieve anxiety and tension. It's great for calming yourself quickly, especially in stressful situations or before bedtime.

How to practice:

- ➢ Sit or lie down in a comfortable position.
- ➢ Inhale through your nose to a count of four.
- ➢ Hold your breath for a count of seven.
- ➢ Exhale through your mouth to a count of eight.
- ➢ Repeat several times, feeling your body relax.

Sound Meditation (Nada Yoga)

Sounds are magical—they surround us everywhere. They can awaken memories, carry us into a dream world, or help us ground ourselves in the present moment. Nada Yoga, an ancient practice of sound meditation, uses the power of sounds to bring the mind into a state of deep peace and harmony. Every sound can become a key to our inner world, promoting relaxation and restoration.

Imagine sitting in a quiet room or in nature. You turn on the sounds of nature: the crashing waves of the ocean, the chirping of birds, the sound of rain, or the gentle chime of bells—or perhaps chanting mantras. You close your eyes, and these sounds, like soft waves, begin to envelop you, penetrating your consciousness. With each passing moment, your mind clings less and less to thoughts and worries, and you begin to simply listen, dissolving into the surrounding sounds.

For those who struggle to focus on silence, sound can serve as an excellent guide into the world of meditation. The sounds around us can not only calm the mind but also open deep inner flows of energy and awareness. Here are a few meditation techniques where sound becomes a vital element of the practice:

- **Meditation on Internal Sound (Antar Nada)**: Focus on the internal sound coming from within your body, such as the pulse of blood or the sound of your breath. Listen to these sounds, letting them lead you to deep relaxation and inner peace.
- **Gong Meditation**: The sound of the gong carries powerful vibrations that help relax the mind and relieve tension. Simply lie down and let the sound of the gong pass through you, feeling its vibrations cleanse your consciousness, bringing inner balance and tranquility.
- **Rain Sound (Binaural Rhythms)**: Rain sounds are natural and soothing melodies that can help you dive into meditation. Play a recording of rain, close your eyes, and imagine the drops softly tapping on the windowpane. Let this sound release your tension and bring you back to a state of peace and harmony.
- **Tibetan Bell Meditation**: Tibetan bells produce clear and melodic sounds that help focus attention and calm the mind.

Play a recording of Tibetan bells or use them in your practice. Let their sound be the center of your attention, clearing your mind of distractions.

- **Whisper of the Wind Meditation**: The whisper of the wind is one of the most pleasant and calming sounds. Find a place in nature where the wind plays with the trees, close your eyes, and let the sound of the wind penetrate your consciousness, as if it's becoming a part of you, bringing a sense of unity with the world.

Meditation on Visualization (Trataka, Visualization)

Trataka is an ancient meditation technique where you focus your gaze on a single object, image, or the flame of a candle, allowing yourself to deeply immerse in it. Eventually, you internalize the image, creating a strong connection between your external and internal worlds.

Meditation through visualization is a powerful technique for those seeking to develop concentration, improve visual perception, and achieve inner calm. Here are several types of visualization meditations, each offering a unique path to harmony and self-discovery:

Trataka on a Candle Flame

Light a candle and focus your attention on its flame. Gradually, try to see the flame within your mind, even with your eyes closed. This strengthens your ability to focus on a single object and clears the mind.

Visualization of a Mountain

This technique uses the image of a majestic mountain to symbolize resilience and tranquility.

- Close your eyes and imagine a tall mountain with a snow-covered peak.
- Feel its stillness and grandeur.
  Allow yourself to become the mountain—steady, confident, and calm, unmoved by the storms of life.
-

34

Visualization of the Ocean

The ocean can symbolize deep emotions and the inner self.

- Imagine sitting by the ocean, watching its waves.
- Each wave represents a thought that comes and goes, but the ocean remains constant.
- You are the ocean—deep and serene.

Mandala Meditation

A mandala is a symbolic design representing the universe.

- Focus on a mandala, either mentally or physically.
- Observe its shape and colors, immersing yourself in its structure.
- Allow yourself to become part of this harmonious circle, experiencing a sense of unity with the cosmos.

Meditation on a Glowing Sphere

This image is used to fill yourself with light and energy.

- Close your eyes and imagine a glowing sphere of bright, pure light above your head.
- The sphere slowly descends, filling your entire body with light and warmth.
- This light cleanses and heals you from within.

Meditation on a Lotus Flower

The lotus is a symbol of spiritual awakening and purity.

Visualize a lotus blooming on a calm water surface.

-

- Its petals open one by one, radiating purity and beauty.
- Feel your mind becoming as pure and clear as this flower.

Visualization of a Sunrise

The sun symbolizes life energy and new beginnings.

- Close your eyes and imagine the sun rising before you.
- With its first rays, your mind fills with light and energy, dispelling all shadows and doubts.
- Feel the renewal and strength brought by each new day.

Meditation on Inner Light

Inner light symbolizes your inner self and true nature.

- Close your eyes and imagine a soft light igniting within your heart.
- The light grows brighter, filling your entire body with warmth and peace.
- You radiate from within, emanating your inner harmony.

Visualization of a Forest

The forest symbolizes unity with nature and the depth of the inner world.

- Close your eyes and imagine walking through a lush, green forest.

  Each step brings you tranquility.

-

- Feel the coolness, hear the rustling leaves, and sense the fresh air.
- In this forest, you find peace and serenity.

These meditations can help you develop creative thinking. Whether you choose an external object or create one in your imagination, each of these techniques will guide you toward inner balance.

Advanced Visualization Meditations

If simple visualization techniques come naturally to you, it's time to explore more complex methods to deepen your practice. You can create more detailed images, such as envisioning light and energy penetrating your body and healing it. Additionally, you can work with multiple levels of consciousness, imagining how your energy connects to the cosmos or an inner source of strength. By forming vivid, intricate images aimed at improving your physical and emotional state, imagine yourself healthy, happy, and harmonious. Feel these qualities filling every cell of your body, gently dissolving all blocks and tension. Sense how the energy of health and harmony spreads throughout your body, filling it with light, strength, and peace.

Meditation on Healing Light

In this meditation, you visualize a stream of healing light entering your body, cleansing it of illnesses and negative energy.

How to practice:

- Sit or lie down in a comfortable position.
- Close your eyes and imagine a bright white light gradually entering your body through the crown of your head.
- This light penetrates every cell, cleansing it of toxins, illnesses, and pain.
- Feel the light filling you with health, energy, and peace.
- Imagine illnesses and tension leaving your body with every exhale.

Meditation on Nature (Grounding and Restoration)

This meditation focuses on restoring health through a connection with nature and grounding.

How to practice:

- Sit or lie down on the ground, preferably outdoors.
- Close your eyes and imagine earth's energy entering your body through the soles of your feet, filling it with strength and health.
- Feel how all negative energy and illnesses leave your body and are absorbed by the earth, where they are transformed and purified.
- Visualize yourself as part of nature, brimming with life energy.

Meditation on Cleansing Inner Light (Energy of Water)

In this technique, visualize water as a symbol of purity cleansing your body and mind from illnesses.

How to practice:

- Imagine standing under a waterfall of clean, sparkling water.
- The water gently and thoroughly washes over you, removing all illnesses, pain, and fatigue.
- Feel the water cleansing every cell of your body, filling you with health and energy.
- Sense the relief and restoration brought by the cleansing process.

Meditation on the Immune System

In this technique, direct your focus on activating and strengthening your immune system.

How to practice:

- Imagine your immune cells (e.g., white blood cells) becoming stronger and more active.
- Visualize them finding and eliminating all threats in your body— viruses, bacteria, and harmful microorganisms.
- Feel your body restoring balance and becoming stronger.

Meditation "The Ideal You"

This meditation helps you visualize yourself at your best— healthy, happy, and successful.

How to practice:

- Sit comfortably, relax, and close your eyes. Take a few deep breaths to calm your mind.

- Imagine your ideal self-standing before you. This person is you at your best—healthy, full of energy, joy, and inner strength.
- Examine this image in detail: how they look, move, and what emotions they radiate. Feel how this ideal selfsmiles, exuding confidence and happiness.

Gradually "merge" this image with yourself with each breath. Visualize this ideal self-blending into you, filling your body with light and energy.

Feel yourself becoming this person. Sense that the health, strength, and harmony of this image are now your reality.

Meditation "Future Happiness"

This meditation focuses on visualizing your happy future. Imagine your life unfolding in the best possible way, and feel happy and harmonious.

How to practice:

- Sit in a comfortable position and close your eyes. Relax.
- Envision yourself traveling forward in time to your future—a future filled with joy, happiness, and success.
- See yourself in this future: how you look, feel, and what you are doing. Imagine every detail as if it is happening right now.

- Feel how the happiness and joy from this future start flowing into your present. This image becomes your reality, and you begin living with this sensation.

Meditation "Golden Stream"

In this meditation, visualize a golden stream of energy cleansing and filling you with strength and harmony.

How to practice:

- Close your eyes and imagine a golden stream of light opening above you.
- This light flows through the crown of your head, filling your entire body, entering every cell.
- Feel how the golden stream washes away all negative emotions and illnesses, leaving only light and health within you.

Meditation "Gratitude"

Focused on visualizing and feeling gratitude, this meditation helps you concentrate on the positive aspects of life.

How to practice:

- Close your eyes and recall moments in life for which you feel gratitude.
- Visualize these moments—people, events, feelings. Feel how gratitude fills your heart and spreads throughout your body.
- Stay in this state of gratitude for as long as you need, enjoying the sense of happiness and harmony.

Meditation "Mirror"

This meditation helps you see your internal state and direct energy toward improving it.

How to Practice:

- Close your eyes and imagine a large mirror in front of you. In this mirror, you see yourself—healthy, happy, and harmonious.
- Look at your reflection and feel how this state becomes real. Every inhale fills you with strength, and every exhale solidifies this state within you.
- Stay in this state, connecting with your reflection, until you feel fully merged with this image.

These are just some of the advanced visualization techniques! Let your imagination guide you—picture yourself standing atop a mountain with energy flowing down from the heavens, enveloping you and spreading around, creating invisible bridges connecting you to every corner of the universe. Envision yourself immersed in an ocean of boundless silence, where water becomes an invisible energy, penetrating every cell and renewing your inner world. Visualize your thoughts turning into bright spheres of light, dancing in harmony with your soul, revealing new horizons of awareness and peace. Don't be afraid to step beyond the ordinary—create unique, profound images that help unlock new opportunities for self-development and harmony.

Chapter 06 Meditation in Daily Life and Relationships

Meditation in Everyday Activities: Cultivating Mindfulness Through Routine

Have you ever wondered why we enjoy immersing ourselves in creative or routine activities like painting, knitting, or fishing? When we focus entirely on these actions, we enter a state of "flow," where the mind tunes out unnecessary worries and concentrates on a single task. This is meditation in everyday action—natural, enjoyable, and accessible to everyone.

These activities bring us back to ourselves. They help us slow down and find inner harmony because meditation isn't only about sitting in silence. It can be any activity that helps anchor attention in the present moment and offers a break from noisy thoughts.

Painting:

Imagine holding a brush and drawing the first stroke on the canvas. At that moment, nothing else exists. You're not thinking about your problems or to-do lists—your entire focus is on the movement of your hand and the blending of colors. This state of deep concentration transforms creativity into meditation. Your mind relaxes, and you simply enjoy the process, immersed in every stroke.

Crafting:

Whether you're sewing, sculpting, or embroidering, pay attention to the texture of the material, the movement of your hands, and how the piece gradually takes shape. This fosters concentration and mindfulness.

Fishing:

Another form of meditation in nature. Sitting by the water, waiting for a fish to bite, your focus is entirely on the present moment. The sound of water, a light breeze, sunlight breaking through the clouds—you simply "are," observing nature and its rhythm. In such moments, you feel part of something greater, bringing deep peace.

Gardening:

While working in the garden, notice the feel of the soil, the smell of plants, and the rustle of leaves in the wind. Immerse yourself in planting, watering, and caring for the plants, acknowledging how each action brings benefit and calms the mind.

Reading:

When reading, focus on each word and its meaning, observing how the text unfolds before you. Allow yourself to become fully absorbed in the book without distractions.

Photography:

While taking photos, concentrate on what you see through the lens. Feel the light, shadows, colors, and composition of the shot. Be present with every moment as you choose the angle and press the shutter, enjoying the process of creating a visual story. ***Culinary Arts:***

If you love baking or experimenting with dishes, focus on every step of the process: the texture of the dough, the aroma of the ingredients, the changing colors of food as it cooks. Be mindful of the fusion of flavors and textures.

Pottery:

While working with clay, notice the sensations as you touch the material and the movement of the pottery wheel. Immerse yourself in shaping the form, observing how the clay changes under your hands.

Cycling:

Riding a bike can be a wonderful mindfulness practice. Focus on the rhythm of your legs, the wind on your face, and the road ahead. Feel the freedom of movement and connection with nature.

Chess:

When playing chess, immerse yourself fully in the decisionmaking process. Be mindful of every move and possible outcome, allowing yourself to remain in the moment of strategic thought.

Dishwashing:

Instead of performing this task mechanically, try focusing on each motion—how your hands move through the water, how the soap bubbles cover the plate, and how the water flows.

Cleaning:

Bring mindfulness into cleaning—notice how you move the broom or vacuum, how you wipe dust and dirt off surfaces. This can turn a routine chore into a way of relaxation and focus.

It's important to fully concentrate on what you're doing and be mindful in every moment. This enables you to experience life more vividly, appreciating its beauty and significance.

By practicing such mindfulness, we begin to notice the beauty in the simplest and most ordinary things that may have once seemed insignificant, giving us the ability to live each moment more deeply and be truly present here and now.

Meditation is a powerful tool that helps establish balance and harmony in various aspects of life. It is a path to selfdiscovery, improved emotional well-being, and deeper connections with others.

In this chapter, we will explore meditative practices that enhance inner harmony and strengthen relationships with loved ones.

Meditation for Inner Harmony: Returning to Yourself

Inner harmony is a quiet, invisible force that sustains us through storms and disagreements. It forms the foundation upon which our entire life is built. When this inner world is calm and balanced, when the soul and body are unified, we can face external challenges with clarity and determination. We not only learn to overcome difficulties but also build healthy, loving, and understanding relationships with those around us.

Here are some of the many meditations that can help you move in this direction:

Loving-Kindness Meditation (Metta Meditation)

This meditation focuses on cultivating unconditional love and kindness toward yourself and others. It helps strengthen compassion, relieve stress, and improve relationships with people.

How to Practice:

- Sit comfortably and close your eyes.
- Repeat phrases directed toward yourself:

  "May I be happy, may I be healthy, may I be safe, may I be at peace."
- Then direct these same wishes toward others: first your loved ones, then acquaintances, and finally those with whom you may have tense relationships.
- Gradually expand this circle of kindness to include the entire world.

Meditation on Death Awareness (Maranasati)

This Buddhist meditation focuses on reflecting on the inevitability of death and the impermanence of existence. It helps manage the fear of death and inspires a more mindful way of living.

How to Practice:

- Sit in a quiet place and focus on the fact that life is finite. • Contemplate your sensations, thoughts, and feelings about death.
- Reflect on how understanding your mortality can transform your state of being.

Pause Before Making an Important Decision

When faced with a tough decision, the first thing to do is stop. A mind overwhelmed by thoughts and emotions rarely leads to the right conclusions. Meditation helps slow down, take a pause, and observe the situation from a distance. This moment of stillness allows us to reconnect with ourselves, our true values, and intuitive decisions.

Below are examples of meditations that can help you make important decisions, gain mental clarity, and stay calm in challenging situations:

Intuitive Meditation (Meditation on Your Inner Voice)

This technique helps you connect with your intuition and inner wisdom, which can provide insights for important decisions. It's particularly helpful when logical analysis doesn't yield an answer, and you feel the need to listen to your inner self.

How to Practice:

- Find a quiet place where you won't be disturbed.
- Sit comfortably, close your eyes, and begin with a few deep breaths to calm your mind.
- Once your mind feels quieter, direct your attention inward.
- Ask yourself a mental question related to the decision you need to make, such as, "What's the best choice for me?" or "What should I do in this situation?"

  Don't try to find an answer immediately. Simply remain in this state, observing thoughts and sensations.
- Allow your inner feeling or image to "surface," guiding you toward the right path.

- After meditating, write down everything you felt or envisioned so you can return to these thoughts and analyze them later.

Visualization of Decision Outcomes

This technique helps you not only analyze all possible options but also see how they would feel in real life. It allows you to envision the final result of each choice and sense which one brings more peace and harmony.

How to Practice:

- Find a quiet place, sit comfortably, and close your eyes.
- Focus on your breathing, gradually relaxing.
- Imagine standing in front of several doors, each representing one of your possible decisions.
- Start with the first door: visualize opening it and stepping into a world where this choice has been implemented.
- Picture yourself a month, a year, or several years after making this decision. How do you feel? What changes have occurred in your life?
- Then move to the next door and repeat the process for the other choices.

-

- After completing the visualization, assess which scenario made you feel the most harmonious and at peace. Your body and mind will guide you toward the decision that offers the greatest clarity and satisfaction.

Detached Observer Meditation (Meditation of the Neutral Witness)

This technique allows you to view a situation without emotional involvement or bias, evaluating it objectively. It enables you to step away from fears and doubts and see the situation in a more neutral light.

How to Practice:

- Sit comfortably, close your eyes, and focus on your breathing.
- Imagine observing yourself from the outside, as though you were another person. See yourself sitting and contemplating the decision at hand.
- Gradually start "watching" the situation that requires your decision, as if you were an external spectator. Visualize the situation as a movie, refraining from becoming emotionally involved. As an observer, consider what advice you'd give this person (yourself) in this situation.
- Pay attention to the feelings and thoughts that arise during this process.

- Conclude the meditation by feeling detached from the situation emotionally, allowing you to approach it with a clear mind.

These meditations help you connect with your intuition and inner wisdom. By applying them before making important decisions, you'll not only make better choices but also feel confident in their correctness

Meditations for Relationships: The Path to Love and Understanding

Relationships with others are an essential part of our lives, like an invisible thread connecting our hearts and souls. They can be a source of joy and support, but they can also create tension and conflict. It is important to remember that each of us is a part of these relationships, and how we treat ourselves influences how we interact with others.

Meditation helps us understand and improve our relationships. By meditating, we learn to be more attentive and understanding, both toward ourselves and those around us. It opens us up to love and compassion, enabling us to better understand the feelings and emotions of others. This can help make our relationships harmonious and supportive.

-

Below, we'll explore various meditations that can help you build relationships with loved ones, friends, colleagues, and even people with whom you've had difficulties.

Heart Connection Meditation

This technique helps strengthen the emotional bond between partners, fostering a sense of unity and harmony. It's perfect for moments when you want to restore closeness and warmth in your relationship.

How to Practice:

- Find a quiet place where you and your partner can meditate together. Sit opposite each other in a comfortable position.
- Close your eyes and begin breathing in sync, trying to align your inhales and exhales.
- Focus on your heart and imagine it filling with light with each breath.
- Visualize this light connecting with your partner's heart.
  With every breath, this connection grows stronger. After a few minutes, imagine your hearts beating as one, sharing love and kindness with each other.
- After the meditation, discuss your experiences to deepen mutual understanding.

Gratitude Meditation for Your Partner

This practice focuses on the positive aspects of your relationship, filling it with gratitude. It can be especially helpful during times of tension or conflict when it's easy to forget what you value in your partner.

How to Practice:

- Sit in a calm setting, close your eyes, and start with a few deep breaths.
- Mentally picture your partner and think about all their positive qualities—whether it's their care, support, love, or other traits you appreciate.
- Silently say phrases like: "I am grateful for you being in my life. I am grateful for all you do for me."
- With each exhale, send love and gratitude toward your partner.
- End the meditation feeling a deep sense of appreciation for your partner and the bond you share.

-

Mindful Touch Meditation

This practice deepens physical and emotional connection through mindful touch. It can strengthen intimacy and improve communication on a physical level.

How to Practice:

- Sit close to your partner or lie down together in a comfortable position.
- Begin by both focusing on your breathing. Breathe deeply and slowly.
- Once relaxed, start gently touching each other's hands or shoulders. Do this mindfully, focusing on the sensations of the touch.
- Notice the emotions that arise during these touches. Feel the warmth, connection, and care emanating from each other.
- Periodically return your attention to your breath while continuing the gentle touches, strengthening both physical and emotional connection.

Shared Goals Meditation

Shared goals and visions of the future can strengthen relationships and steer them in a positive direction. This technique helps you visualize a future together, fostering mutual understanding and trust.

How to Practice:

- Sit together in a quiet place and start the meditation with deep breathing.
- Close your eyes and imagine your shared future. How do you see your relationship in one year, five years, or ten years?
- Visualize moments of joy, success, shared achievements, and how you support each other in this future.
- Imagine yourselves overcoming challenges together, finding solutions, and supporting each other during difficult times.
- After the meditation, discuss your feelings and visions of the future to better understand each other's expectations and goals.

Conflict Mindfulness Meditation

When conflict arises in a relationship, it's essential to pause and recognize your emotions to avoid escalating the situation. This technique helps cultivate mindfulness during conflicts and find a path to reconciliation.

How to Practice:

- When emotions run high during an argument, take a pause and ask your partner to stop for a moment.
- Close your eyes and focus on your breathing. Take a few deep inhales and exhales to calm your body and mind.

- Acknowledge your emotions—whether anger, hurt, or frustration. Don't suppress them; simply observe them.
- Once calm, return to the conversation with your partner, expressing your feelings calmly and mindfully.
- Discuss your emotions and try to understand each other's perspectives to find a path to mutual understanding and reconciliation.

Trust-Building Meditation

Trust is the foundation of any strong relationship. This meditation helps open the heart and create an atmosphere of safety and support.

How to Practice:

- Sit facing your partner. Hold hands and close your eyes. • Begin breathing in sync, feeling each other's warmth and presence.
- Mentally repeat phrases like: "I trust you. I am ready to support and be open with you."
- Visualize your hearts connecting, with trust growing stronger between you.
- Stay in this state for a few minutes, feeling a deep sense of connection and safety.

Forgiveness Meditation for Parents (Mother or Father)

Relationships with parents can be complex, especially if there have been past grievances or misunderstandings. Forgiveness meditation helps release old wounds and improve your bond with your mother or father.

How to Practice:

- Find a quiet place and sit in a calm posture.
- Close your eyes and take deep breaths, focusing on your breath.
- Visualize your parent—your mother or father—standing before you.
- Silently say: "I forgive you for everything that has happened between us. I release all grievances and allow our connection to improve."
- Imagine your heart filling with light and love, directing these feelings toward your parent.
- Try to maintain this feeling of forgiveness and acceptance in future interactions.

Tolerance Meditation for Your Boss

Relationships with a boss can be a source of stress. Tolerance meditation helps cultivate understanding and calmness at work, reducing stress and improving professional relationships. **How to Practice:**

- Find a quiet place to sit and relax. Close your eyes and take deep breaths.
- Visualize your boss standing before you.
- Silently say: "I accept you as you are. May our professional relationship be filled with understanding and respect".
- If negative emotions arise, don't fight them—just observe and release them, returning to a state of calm.
- Imagine your interactions improving and finding common ground with your boss.

Forgiveness Meditation for Enemies or Conflicted Relationships

Relationships with enemies or those you have conflicts with can evoke strong negative emotions. Forgiveness and release meditation helps free yourself from these feelings and restore inner peace.

How to Practice:

- Sit in a quiet place, close your eyes, and focus on your breathing.
- Recall a person you have a conflict with or consider an enemy.
- Silently say: "I forgive you for everything that has happened between us. I release this grievance and free myself from negative emotions."
- Imagine your heart filling with light and kindness, dissolving all negativity.
- End the meditation with a sense of relief and peace.

Chapter 07 Transcendental Meditation: The Path to the Divine

Immersion into the Transcendental State

All the previous meditations have been aimed at calming the mind, overcoming stress, cultivating inner harmony, and strengthening relationships. Transcendental meditation, however, takes us to a realm where the boundaries between "self" and the world, between mind and spirit, dissolve. It is a journey into a state where all conventional divisions—inner and outer, material and immaterial—become irrelevant. We enter a space where only pure consciousness exists, and in this state, we begin to realize our inseparable connection with the Divine. This is a place free from attachments and thoughts, where we perceive the world as a unified, infinite, and deeply harmonious whole.

Unlike other meditative practices, transcendental meditation is focused on transcending all limitations and merging with the Source that underlies all existence.

Mantras: The Key to Deep Awareness

The primary tool of transcendental meditation is **mantras**— sacred sound vibrations used in spiritual practices to focus the mind and achieve a profound state of awareness. These mantras serve as a bridge to connect with the Divine. They carry a unique power, penetrating deeply into the mind and body, bringing transformative effects that guide the practitioner to experience unity with higher energies and the spiritual realm.

Unlike other techniques, mantra meditation centers on Divine sounds or sacred imagery. These sounds have no material meaning, but their vibrations reach deep into the consciousness, helping us attain transcendence. Mantra meditation is a journey of profound awareness, leading to spiritual awakening. Whenever the mind begins to wander, the mantra gently redirects focus to the inner space, keeping the consciousness present and connected to higher realities.

Some forms of mantra meditation involve visualizing sacred images associated with Divine aspects. These images are not just visual representations; they are symbols through which one can attune to the Divine presence. As you visualize these images, the mantra becomes amplified, connecting you to higher energies through both sound and visual imagery. This leads to the realization that the true nature of our being is not the material body, thoughts, or emotions, but pure consciousness, inherently connected to the Supreme. This transcendental state reveals our deep unity with the Divine.

This experience cannot be described in words, as it lies beyond the realm of mind and speech. It is akin to enlightenment, where there is no separation between the "self" and the "external world." At this moment, we realize that the Divine is not "out there" somewhere—it has always been and will always be a part of us. We are not separate from it; we are its manifestation.

When we immerse ourselves in transcendental meditation, it feels like "returning home" to our original state of purity and light. In this state, there is no fear, no anxiety, no desire to change or achieve anything. There is only a profound, blissful experience of unity with the Divine. This state, often called **samadhi** in spiritual teachings, is described as the ultimate goal of life.

Examples of Transcendental Mantras

Each mantra is a key to profound inner states, a vibration connecting us to the Divine. Here are some mantras, each with its unique power:

- **OM** – The primordial sound of the universe, symbolizing all existence.
- **AUM NAMO NARAYANAYA** – A salutation to Lord Narayana, the preserver of the universe.
- **OM MANI PADME HUM** – "Oh, precious lotus, grant me purity and wisdom."
- **OM NAMO BHAGAVATE VASUDEVAYA** – A salutation to Lord Vasudeva, the embodiment of love and truth.
- **OM SHRI GANESHAYA NAMAH** – A salutation to Lord Ganesha, the remover of obstacles.
- **GAYATRI MANTRA** – "We meditate on the glory of the one who created this universe. May he guide our mind to the righteous path"

- **OM NAMAH SHIVAYA** – A salutation to Lord Shiva, the symbol of transformation and liberation.
- **OM SHRI MAHA LAKSHMIYAI NAMAH –** A salutation to Goddess Lakshmi, who grants abundance and harmony.
- **OM TAT SAT** – "That is the Truth."
- **OM GURU DEVA NAMAH** – A salutation to the spiritual teacher, the guide to wisdom.
- **OM AIM SARASVATYAI NAMAH** – A salutation to Goddess Saraswati, the patroness of knowledge and the arts.

How to Practice:
- *Choose a Mantra:* Select a mantra that resonates with your heart and aligns with your intention.
- *Create a Sacred Space:* Find a place where you can be alone, free from external distractions.
- *Sit Comfortably:* Sit with a straight spine in a posture that you can maintain for an extended period.
- *Relax and Breathe:* Close your eyes, relax your body, and allow your breath to flow naturally.
- *Repeat the Mantra:* Begin repeating your chosen mantra, either mentally or aloud, synchronizing it with your breath.
- *Focus on the Sound:* Let the vibrations of the mantra cleanse your consciousness and fill your body with harmony.

- **Gently Refocus:** If your mind starts to wander, gently bring your attention back to the sound of the mantra.
- **Immerse Yourself:** Allow the practice to guide you into a state of silence and awareness.

Let this practice serve as your guide to the world of tranquility and mindfulness. Each mantra carries a unique power to lead you toward deep transformational experiences. As you continue on this journey, may you experience the profound bliss and unity that transcendental meditation offers.

Chapter 08 The Power of Sacred Names: A Simple Practice for Deep Transformation

The Vedic texts are the oldest and most sacred scriptures of humanity, containing profound knowledge about life, the universe, and spirituality. They encompass all aspects of human existence, offering an understanding of the laws of the universe as well as a path to spiritual growth and enlightenment. They view meditation as a means to delve deeper into reality and one's true nature.

The Bhagavad Gita on Meditation

One of the most important texts describing the path of meditation is the **Bhagavad Gita**. The Bhagavad Gita, which translates as "The Song of God," holds a central place among all Vedic scriptures and serves as a spiritual guide revealing eternal truths. The Gita covers numerous aspects of life: from understanding one's nature and purpose to attaining the highest state of awareness and unity with the Divine. It is a key to understanding the entirety of Vedic wisdom, as it contains the fundamental principles laid out in all the sacred texts.

Krishna in the Gita offers universal solutions for various life situations, addressing each individual uniquely. This makes the text relevant throughout the ages. The Bhagavad Gita explores topics such as *karma* (action), *bhakti* (devotion), **jnana** (knowledge), and *raja-yoga* (the path of realization), integrating them into a unified teaching of spiritual development.

This great song teaches the art of living consciously, embracing one's duties, understanding one's true self, and finding connection with the highest reality. For this reason, it is called the essence of all Vedic philosophy and a spiritual guide for all times.

This unique text is a dialogue between Krishna and Arjuna, which takes place on the battlefield of Kurukshetra. Arjuna, a great warrior and prince, faces an internal crisis on the battlefield, torn by doubts and uncertainty. He is to fight against his relatives and teachers, and this moral conflict paralyzes him. At this moment, Krishna, his friend and mentor, the incarnation of the Supreme Personality of God on Earth who appeared 5,000 years ago, begins to explain profound philosophical truths to Arjuna.

Krishna reveals to him the path to inner liberation through meditation and focus. In the Bhagavad Gita, Krishna explains the fundamentals of *dhyana-yoga*—the yoga of meditation— teaching how to control the mind, overcome attachments, and achieve unity with the Divine. Krishna advises Arjuna: *"Let the yogi concentrate the mind, controlling thoughts and desires, sitting straight in a secluded place, and thus achieve the highest state of peace."*

Krishna explains that a true yogi is one who remains in the world while maintaining focus and purity of mind. Meditation helps to rid oneself of attachments and inner conflicts, leading to *samadhi*—a state of deep unity with the Divine.

The Bhagavad Gita not only teaches philosophy but also provides practical recommendations for life, showing how meditation and self-discovery can lead to wisdom and harmony. It emphasizes that meditation helps to perceive everything as a manifestation of the highest reality.

A Journey Through Ages: The Transformation of Meditation

To understand how meditation has transformed and why mantra meditation has become the most important practice of our time, let us take a journey through the ages—from the Golden Age of *Satya Yuga*, through the eras of rituals and worship, up to the present **Kali Yuga.** In each of these eras, meditation played its special role, and its methods were revealed according to the spiritual needs of humanity.

Looking into the past, we will see how the forms and methods of meditation evolved and how mantra meditation in Kali Yuga becomes a saving anchor in a world of spiritual degradation.

The Vedic scriptures describe the cyclic nature of time through the concept of four **yugas**—ages, each with its own characteristics and level of spiritual development of humanity. Each yuga required its unique ways of interacting with the Divine, corresponding to the level of awareness and spiritual purity of the people of that time.

Satya Yuga: The Age of Purity and Perfect Meditation

Satya Yuga, also known as the "Golden Age," was the first and longest era. It was characterized by absolute spiritual purity and harmony between man and the cosmos. People at this time were so pure that their minds easily focused on the Divine without any distractions. Meditation in Satya Yuga was a natural state of consciousness.

In Satya Yuga, people meditated on *Brahman*—the infinite, impersonal essence that permeates all existence. They could enter a state of *samadhi*—complete unity with the Divine— remaining in this state for many years or even centuries.

They lived in harmony with nature, in simplicity and focus, and their inner world was a reflection of the external harmony of the universe.

Treta Yuga: The Era of Rituals and Worship

Treta Yuga, following Satya Yuga, introduced slightly more complex conditions for meditation. People still possessed a high degree of spirituality, but the material reality became more pronounced, and maintaining a spiritual state required greater effort. Meditation became less accessible and necessitated additional rituals and forms of worship.

In Treta Yuga, the primary spiritual practice was fire sacrifices (yajnas), performed to maintain a connection with the gods and the universe. Sages conducted these rituals with absolute precision, using the power of mantras and meditation to invoke the blessings of the gods. Fire, as a symbol of purification and transformation, became the central element of spiritual practices.

People of this era had strong concentration abilities, but achieving the state of **samadhi** required more time and effort compared to Satya Yuga.

Dvapara Yuga: The Era of Worshiping Divine Forms

In Dvapara Yuga, as material reality became even more prominent, spiritual practices grew increasingly complex. People of this era lost a portion of their spiritual purity, and their minds became more susceptible to distractions and desires. Maintaining a connection with the Divine was no longer achievable through simple meditation on

Brahman or rituals alone. Instead, Dvapara Yuga ushered in the worship of specific forms of God—Divine avatars and manifestations became the focal point of spiritual practices.

During this time, meditation shifted increasingly towards *bhakti,* or devotional service to God. People meditated on the images and forms of various avatars, such as Krishna, Vishnu, Rama, and others. Practices included not only internal contemplation but also active forms of worship, such as singing sacred names. Meditation on the form of the Divine became the central spiritual practice of the era.

Mantras also played a crucial role in the meditation practices of Dvapara Yuga. Unlike earlier epochs, where meditation was more about internal states, Dvapara Yuga emphasized external worship and the regular repetition of mantras to maintain spiritual purity.

Kali Yuga: The Era of Mantras

Kali Yuga, the age in which we currently live according to Vedic tradition, is the final epoch of the four Yugas that alternate in cycles of creation. While earlier ages were characterized by harmony, righteousness, and spiritual purity, Kali Yuga is marked by the degradation of human values, an increase in conflicts, and a growing disconnection from the Divine. It is an age where material pleasures are prioritized over spiritual goals, and human consciousness becomes increasingly clouded by illusions of ego, desires, and fears.

The signs of this age are evident everywhere: the pursuit of power and wealth overshadows compassion and love, aggression and envy undermine harmony in relationships, and the relentless race for success silences the inner voice of truth.

Traditional spiritual practices that once helped people maintain their connection with the Divine now demand far greater effort and discipline.

In earlier ages, spiritual practices were a natural part of daily life. People's minds were calm, their bodies resilient, and they could meditate for years, maintaining high levels of concentration and inner peace. However, in Kali Yuga, where life moves at a frantic pace and the world is filled with noise and distractions, classical meditations, such as deep concentration or prolonged visualizations, have become nearly unattainable for the modern individual.

Modern culture, built on constant stimulation and distraction, makes it difficult to cultivate focus. People are accustomed to living in a state of multitasking, with minds oscillating between countless thoughts, unable to find peace. Classical meditation techniques, which require prolonged focus, have become especially challenging in an environment where our minds are perpetually "noisy."

Daily stress disrupts the inner balance necessary for deep meditation. The constant tension of mind and body makes it harder to enter a state of calm and concentration.

Kali Yuga is a time when people are increasingly absorbed in material concerns, losing interest in spiritual matters. The focus on external achievements hinders the development of inner life and makes meditation even more difficult. Yet, it is precisely during this time that the need for meditation is greater than ever before. People need a practice to help them cope with daily challenges, manage their minds, calm their emotions, and restore their connection to the spiritual source.

Meditation becomes a lifeline, helping individuals avoid drowning in the sea of chaos.

However, accessible and effective tools are needed for daily application. Meditation today is not just a path to enlightenment but a means of survival in the face of emotional and mental overload.

The Power of Sound: Salvation in the Age of Kali Yuga

In the dark period of Kali Yuga, a force foretold by ancient sages reveals itself—a force that offers clarity and connection amidst the chaos. This force is sound meditation, specifically mantra meditation, described as one of the most powerful practices available in our era. This transformative practice was brought to the world by Lord Chaitanya, a great saint and spiritual teacher who appeared 500 years ago with a profound mission. He came to provide humanity with a simple, accessible means of purifying the mind and immersing oneself in transcendental consciousness, even amidst the challenges and limitations of Kali Yuga.

Lord Chaitanya: The Greatest Advocate of Mantra Meditation

Lord Chaitanya is one of the most remarkable avatars to have descended into this world during our epoch. His role in spreading spiritual wisdom and meditation is unparalleled. He appeared as the embodiment of the highest form of love and compassion, being both Divine and human at the same time.

Chaitanya introduced a simple yet profoundly powerful method of connecting with the Divine—repeating the holy name. He taught that the truth about the Divine is not hidden in complex rituals or philosophical concepts but in devotion, love, and the chanting of the holy name. In his teachings, Lord Chaitanya placed the mantra "Hare Krishna, Hare Rama" at the center of all spiritual practices, asserting that through the repetition of this mantra, anyone can enter transcendental consciousness and experience a direct connection with the Supreme.

The significance of the "Hare Krishna" mantra lies in its simplicity and accessibility to everyone, regardless of their background or societal status, as a way to attain inner peace and direct communion with the Divine. Lord Chaitanya taught that this path—a path of love—remains accessible to all despite the challenges of Kali Yuga.

Lord Chaitanya declared that in Kali Yuga, meditation on sacred sounds (mantras) is the simplest and most effective method of spiritual purification and enlightenment. He emphasized that the constant repetition of the mantra can swiftly cleanse the mind of impurities, dissolve anxieties, and restore a person's natural state of awareness and harmony.

Unlike complex visualization techniques or prolonged meditative practices, mantra meditation is simple to perform and does not require intricate physical or mental efforts. Its power lies in sound.

The continual repetition of sacred sounds helps dispel worries, cleanse the mind, and tune it to higher frequencies. We can chant the mantra at any time of the day—while working, walking, or resting. There is no need for special conditions, making it ideal for those living in the hustle and bustle of modern life.

This mantra uncovers profound levels of consciousness, restoring lost connections with the Divine. Its regular repetition penetrates the deep layers of subconscious blocks that hinder spiritual growth.

Lord Chaitanya stated that in Kali Yuga, there is no more powerful method of purification and reconnection with the Divine than the practice of mantra meditation.

The Impact of Mantra Meditation on Modern Culture and Society

Hare Krishna meditation has had, and continues to have, a profound influence on modern culture and society. From its introduction in the West during the 1960s, this practice has become a cultural phenomenon, reaching various layers of society, from musicians to politicians, from workers to spiritual seekers.

The influence of the Hare Krishna movement is particularly evident in music culture. As mentioned earlier, George Harrison incorporated mantras into his compositions, such as "My Sweet Lord," which became a spiritual anthem for an entire generation. The sounds of the holy names on records spinning worldwide touched the hearts of people and helped many discover profound spiritual experiences.

The hippie movement of the '60s and '70s, initially focused on material pleasures, was quickly transformed under the influence of Eastern philosophies, with the Hare Krishna movement playing a significant role. Chanting the mantra became a bridge connecting young people seeking genuine spiritual experience with ancient culture and its profound truths. Hare Krishna became associated with liberation from material bonds, the pursuit of purity, and true love, leaving an indelible mark on global culture.

In recent decades, Hare Krishna meditation has gained broad recognition in the field of spiritual psychology and personal growth. The practice of mantra repetition has become part of personal development programs and spiritual awakening workshops offered both in Western countries and in India. People working on their emotional and psychological challenges find in this practice a simple yet powerful method for transforming consciousness and strengthening inner resilience.

The strength of the Hare Krishna mantra meditation lies in its universality. It is not tied to any specific cultural context or religious tradition. This practice is open to everyone, regardless of where they live, their social status, or their beliefs. Mantra meditation is accessible and sought after by those seeking spiritual depth and inner harmony.

People worldwide find it a way to overcome inner conflicts and achieve peace of mind. For example, in Latin American countries such as Brazil and Argentina, Hare Krishna meditation has spread widely among youth who are disillusioned with modern society and are searching for deeper meaning in life.

In Europe, particularly in countries like the United Kingdom, Germany, and France, devotees have organized numerous festivals where collective chanting of the mantra becomes a means of uniting people, creating an atmosphere of love and friendship. These vibrant cultural events attract thousands of participants.

The practice of Hare Krishna has become a powerful source of spiritual energy for millions worldwide. It allows everyone to realize their connection with the world, gain spiritual wisdom, and begin living more consciously and harmoniously.

The Holy Name: A Guide to Spiritual Transformation

The holy name of God is not merely a sound vibration. According to Vedic texts, the holy name of God is nondifferent from God Himself. When we chant the "Hare Krishna" mantra, we are literally inviting the Divine presence into our lives.

Chanting the holy names has a profound purifying effect. Our mind gradually becomes calmer and more focused. The mantra cleanses it of negative thoughts, grudges, fears, and material desires that obscure our true nature and helps it focus on the Supreme. We begin to feel an inner joy. Gradually, anger, envy, and anxiety fade away, replaced by a deep sense of love and gratitude.

Chanting the holy names allows us to deepen our awareness of our connection with God and understand that we are eternal souls, and our true happiness cannot be found in external circumstances. With each repetition of the mantra, we gradually free ourselves from material suffering. The mantra helps us quickly realize that we are not part of this material world and reconnects us with our true spiritual selves.

This path is open to anyone willing to accept the mantra as their spiritual practice. Regardless of where you are, your age, or your faith, chanting the holy names can transform your life and free you from inner suffering.

The Uniqueness of the "Hare Krishna" Mantra

The mantra "Hare Krishna, Hare Krishna, Krishna Krishna, Hare Hare, Hare Rama, Hare Rama, Rama Rama, Hare Hare" is not merely a sequence of sounds but powerful vibrations carrying immense transcendental potency.

Hare refers to the divine energy of the Supreme, embodied in Srimati Radharani, the highest form of love and devotion. Her energy helps cleanse the heart and awaken love for God. **Krishna** is the name of God, meaning "All-Attractive." Chanting this name connects a person to the source of all existence and helps realize their connection with the Divine.

Rama is another name of God, meaning "Inner Bliss." Repeating this name immerses one in a state of spiritual bliss and peace.

Chanting the holy names of God acts like a purifying rain that washes away all impurities from the surface of the mind and heart. The "Hare Krishna" mantra functions like water that cleanses the dust of material concerns, returning us to our true spiritual nature. Repeating the holy names helps dispel unnecessary thoughts, fears, and desires. The mantra cleanses the heart, opening it to Divine love and joy. You begin to feel that your happiness resides within you and is independent of external circumstances.

Types and Techniques of Mantra Meditation: Japa, Kirtan, and Harinama

Now that we understand the profound spiritual power of the mantra and its influence on the mind, we can move to the practical aspect: how to meditate using the holy names. Below are several types of mantra meditation that deepen our consciousness and strengthen our connection with the Divine.

Japa (Personal Meditation with the Mantra)

Japa is one of the most common forms of mantra meditation. It involves repeating the mantra either aloud or silently. Typically, a string of 108 beads is used to keep track of repetitions, ensuring focus on the process. Japa is a solitary practice that helps concentrate the mind on the sound of the mantra, cleansing it of external distractions.

How to Practice Japa:
1. Find a quiet place where you will not be disturbed.
2. Take a set of beads (japa mala) and begin chanting the "Hare Krishna" mantra or another sacred mantra.
3. Move one bead at a time with each repetition of the mantra.
4. Gradually, you will feel your mind becoming focused and calm.
5. Pause between repetitions to feel the inner resonance.

Kirtan (Collective Chanting)

Kirtan is a form of meditation where people come together to chant the holy names in a group setting. During kirtan, music and singing become tools that help each participant reach a state of deep inner peace. The mantra is repeated over and over, capturing the minds and hearts of everyone involved. Bodies begin to move to the rhythm, and this is not just dancing—it is an expression of the joy that comes from connecting with the Divine.

People forget their worries, daily struggles, and distractions as their hearts fill with love and harmony. In these moments, everyone participating in kirtan feels a connection to something greater than themselves.

How to Practice Kirtan:
1. Gather with friends or fellow devotees.
2. The leader begins singing the mantra, and everyone else repeats it.
3. Open your heart, allowing the sounds to penetrate you and fill your consciousness with light and joy.

Kirtan amplifies spiritual energy, creating an atmosphere of inner enlightenment and happiness. This collective practice cleanses the consciousness of the entire group, strengthening a sense of community and spiritual connection.

What happens when kirtan steps out of temples and homes? When devotees take to the streets with the mantra on their lips, it becomes harinama—a moving meditation that can be encountered anywhere in the world.

Imagine walking down the street of a bustling metropolis, immersed in your endless tasks, when suddenly you hear the rhythmic sounds of the mantra accompanied by the beat of drums and the chime of cymbals. You see people dancing and singing with such joy that their energy begins to spread to those around them.

People in vibrant attire walk through city streets, filling them with sacred sounds. They bring not just music but vibrations that purify the mind and the atmosphere.

Harinama:

Harinama becomes a living mantra, spreading harmony and joy to the heart of anyone who hears it. The most remarkable part is that anyone passing by can join in. There's no need to be a scholar of the Vedas or an experienced meditator—just open your heart and start chanting the mantra.

Today, such groups of devotees can be found all over the world: from New York to Tokyo, from London to Mumbai. Chanting the holy names takes place in parks, on squares, by rivers and lakes, and anyone can become part of this spiritual movement. Chanting the mantra becomes accessible to all, regardless of religion, age, or social status.

Harinama serves as a vibrant reminder that liberation and spiritual awakening can be experienced right here, amidst the noise and bustle of our daily lives.

Chapter 09 Practical Tips for Building a Sustainable Daily Practice

In this book, we've explored many aspects of meditation: its types, goals, and the profound ways it can transform our lives. We've come to understand that meditation is a powerful tool for achieving inner peace, improving health, and fostering spiritual growth. However, for many beginners, meditation might seem either simple or dauntingly out of reach. In this chapter, we'll look at how to make meditation a natural part of your life.

Tips for Building a Sustainable Daily Practice
Start Small

Begin with small steps—just 5–10 minutes a day. This will feel manageable and allow you to gradually integrate meditation into your life without overwhelming yourself.

Set a Specific Time for Meditation

Habits form more easily when anchored to a particular time of day. Choose a time that works best for you and stick to it every day. It could be in the morning before starting your day or in the evening before bedtime.

Use Triggers

Triggers are actions or events that remind you to meditate. For instance, waking up, having breakfast, or turning off your phone in the evening can serve as signals to begin your practice.

Create a Meditation Space

Having a designated space for meditation helps you enter a focused and calm state more quickly. It doesn't need to be an entire room—just a cozy corner where you feel comfortable and won't be disturbed.

Use Apps or Reminders

There are many apps available that can help you remember to meditate and support you in building the habit. Some even include short guided meditations and reminders to encourage daily practice.

Don't Punish Yourself for Missed Sessions

Forming a habit is a gradual process, and there may be days when you miss your practice. Avoid criticizing yourself for it. The key is to return to your practice the next day and continue rather than giving up because of one missed session.

Gradually Increase the Duration

Start with short sessions and slowly extend the time as meditation becomes a natural part of your day. Don't force yourself to meditate for long periods immediately—let the duration grow naturally as you feel ready.

Make Meditation Part of Your Lifestyle

Meditation shouldn't feel like a chore or an obligation. Try to see it as a pleasant ritual—a time for yourself to relax, recharge, and reconnect.

Conclusion

Throughout this book, we have delved into the world of meditation—an ancient practice that has inspired people for countless ages to seek peace, harmony, and a connection with the Divine. We have explored its philosophy, practical applications, and scientific foundations, discovering how it transforms lives and learning ways to integrate it into our everyday routines.

Meditation is a path to freedom. It empowers us to live each day with love and mindfulness. It liberates us from illusions and teaches us to embrace life in all its diversity. Every moment of mindfulness cleanses our minds from the noise of the world and our hearts from fear. Meditation reminds us that happiness and harmony do not come from the outside—they are already within us.

Every moment spent in meditation is a step toward inner peace, where calm, love, and clarity prevail.

Remember, every time you sit down to meditate, you contribute to creating a space of awareness and harmony that gradually transforms the world around you. The mindfulness of one person can inspire many, filling the world with light and kindness.

May this book serve as a starting point for a meaningful life, and may your meditation practice bring clarity, enrich your life with purpose, and strengthen your connection with yourself, the Higher Power, and the Divine.

Use this knowledge to open the door to freedom and happiness in the present moment. Begin the journey within yourself, and you will see how the outer world starts to reflect your inner reality, filling it with harmony, light, and love.

And remember: everything you need is already within you. Simply pause, feel the silence, and allow yourself to be. Take your time, enjoy every moment, and uncover new horizons of your inner world.

This is your path. This is your life. And it is worthy of being lived mindfully, with wisdom and love!

Printed in Great Britain
by Amazon